Andrea Regina Katharina InEssenz

The Spiritual Condition of the World

Translated from German
by Vincenzo Benestante

Table of Contents

Andrea Regina Katharina InEssenz

The Spiritual Condition of the World

Foreword

The world is a distinct product created by the human spirit, which - having been caused to fall by original sin - is meant to expose this world of deception and to dress it in the spiritual clothing of God.

As it is in heaven, so shall it be on Earth. As Jesus taught us in the Lord's Prayer, „Hallowed be thy name".

The implementation of that in all life's time is the spiritual medicine for this world.

Without God, we are impoverished in spirit. Return to your original wealth. Jesus will lead you; follow his footsteps.
So be it.

Spiritual man

The human spirit is coupled with the body of flesh, the body of emotion, and with the mental body. The mind, free will and experiences are situated in the soul body.

When considering the length of time in which we must return again and again in order to experience, to recognise, and to illuminate what we recognise, it becomes clear, that we are bound in the spirit and in the soul. This spiritual bond affects all seven bodies of the human being. Further, it also affects the body of community here on Earth; which is to say it affects the collective, including all of nature and the animal world.

The bound spirit acts out of the world of experience and develops out of this law. Therefore, the human being hardly moves forward at all, but rather continues to do his/her laps on a carousel of birth and death.

Some spirits actually free themselves out of this bondage and expand – beyond the material realm.

Here, however, life-threatening spiritual danger also exists. The spirit which expands outward needs a compass, in order to grow into the good spiritual worlds; and this compass is the Word of Jesus to mankind.

The directional words can be found by concentrating on the Sermon on the Mount. Without a compass, the escaped spirit will land in the world of seduction by demons and evil sorts of beings.

This has happened to humankind since the birth of original sin through Eve.

Our lifespan

What we have all grasped, is that time is limited and transitory. It does not persist; it absorbs vitality and uses it up. Thus it is virtually natural, that even time itself is limited and will end.

And now this is happening: the time of mankind is coming to an end. The period of grace, during which mankind could run riot and test itself, so to speak, is over. The spiritual chaos in the hereafter must be brought back into proper order; and each spirit returned to the correct state of existence.

This process cannot be avoided and is unstoppable. God's patience ends now – as well as his emanations into all people, who have dulcified their actions. The rampant spirit of mankind produced terrible things during the times of its mode of life. If God's spirit in the form of the power of grace had not come over this world, mankind would have destroyed itself. Even all animals and the entirety of nature would have fallen victim to it.

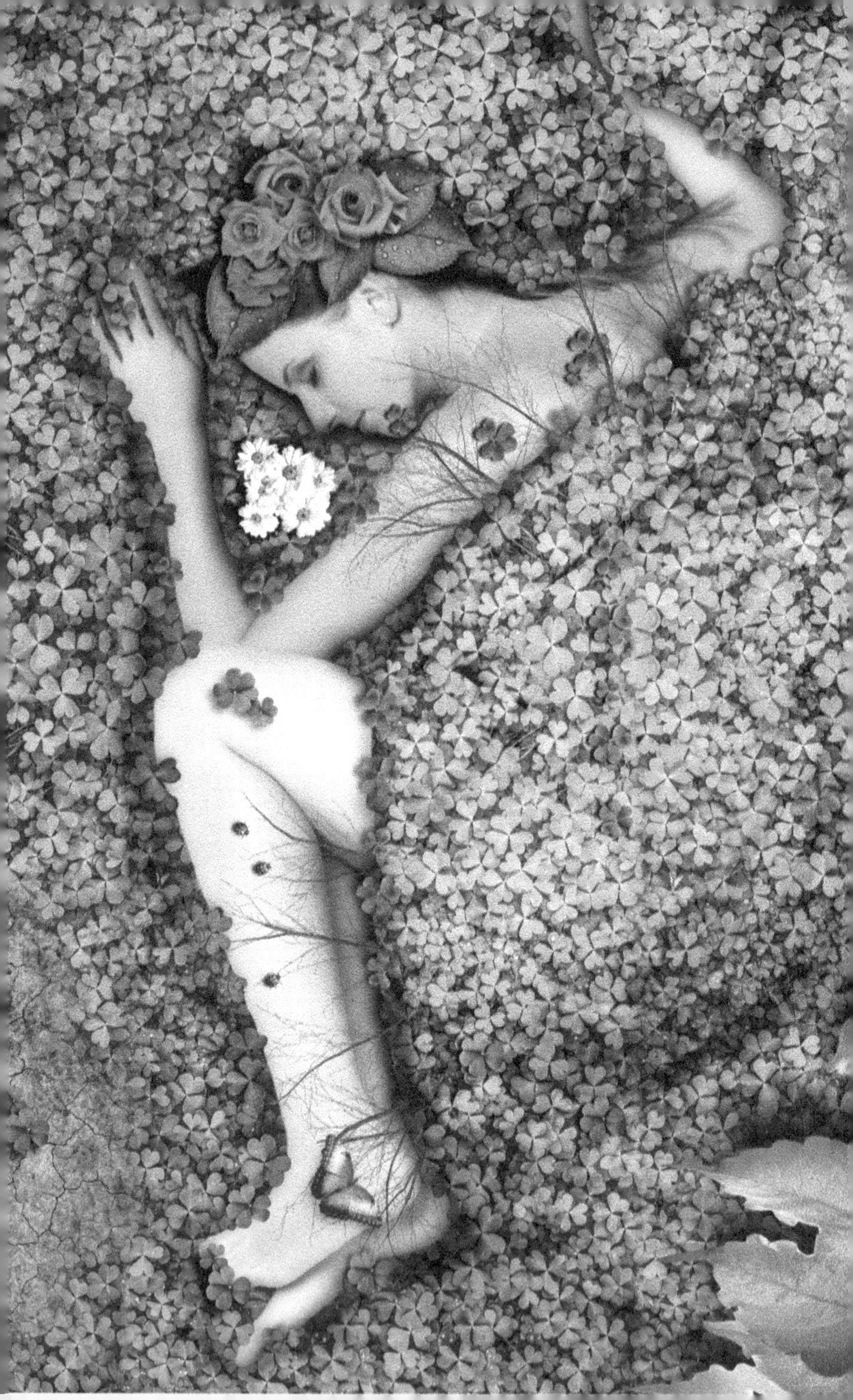

Now this comes to an end. God now demands a spiritual decision from mankind. He says, „Come home, in my house there are many mansions".

If we do not accept this invitation, we will be forever as lost as we are today. Without God there can be no peace in the soul. It has been dragged through time fully burdened with impure undergrowth far too long.

Let us summarise and ask ourselves this question:

Why is mankind in this state of unrest?

The answer: the separation from God, from the heavenly state of being has far-reaching CONSEQUENCES!

There is a primal reason, a primal cause responsible for the condition which is now lived and experienced:

The so-called first disobedience by Eve and Adam. God instructed them how to comport themselves in Paradise according to His righteous Will. Eve, however, ignored this and followed the voice (the snake) of the greatest enemy of God – the devil! In this she interrupted the basic trust of her creator and the virtuous relationship with him. She followed the primal source of evil and seduction.

This is the original catastrophe, from which stem all catastrophes of the collective, as well as of the individual. Every form of misery and suffering, regardless of the type, stems from this primal misdeed. All types of torment accompany mankind, who “wanted to be like God”.

Modern man is the descendant of Eve and Adam and lives in this world under the influence of evil for that reason. He, the devil, hates God above all things and uses humans as tools to weaken God and to take over - and own - God‘s Creation.

It should not surprise us, that the Earth is saturated with misery and plagued by many catastrophes. Wars, acts of atrocity such as rape and murder, hunger and many schisms and blasphemies stem from this godless relationship. Corruption and deceit hold sway here. Evil hypnotises the spirit of mankind and pulls us down, away from love and peace.

It is therefore clearly up to us; we decide always, what we want to be; and if we live without God, we will always remain virtually lost in time.

What is happening to mankind?

Now the door to the past is closed. Evil; the devil, who has elevated himself through sin as king of this world, suspects that God is now forcing mankind to make a decision. Many souls have gained knowledge during the course of their last ten lifetimes and have thereby experienced release from numerous wounds.

This spiritual illumination angers Evil and it concentrated its powers of seduction to produce poison. The devil introduced this poison into the spirits of human beings, instilling love-drops and new-Earth drops as well - but only minute amounts; just enough to make the potion effective, but not strong enough for the poison to be deadly. The addition of the love-drops is a cunning act, which holds people to the belief that they are moving about within the healthy light of God. Thus they believe they can free themselves from all errors which are within the soul and in the spiritual. We see how hideously the Dark operates and how important it is in this world, that all people go with Jesus to God. But how can this be accomplished, what must we do?

What can help mankind?

The answer: God gave us explicit instructions in his word, as to how we are to live for him. That includes:

- The command to love one another.
- The call to follow him, disregarding our personal wishes.
- Urging us to care for the poor and needy.
- The warning, not to fall into sinful comportment, as do those who do not know God.

Jesus summed up a life for God, when a teacher of the law asked him about the most important commandment. *„Jesus answered: The highest commandment is this: ‚Hear, Israel, the Lord, our God is the sole Lord, and you shall love the Lord, your God with all your heart, with all your soul, with your entire mind and with all your strength.' The other is this: ‚You shall love your neighbour as yourself.' There is no other commandment greater than these."*

Mark 12, 29-31

The prayer of Jesus before his crucifixion also sheds light on the meaning of our life. In reference to believers he prays:

"And I have given them the glory, which you gave me, so that they may be one, as we are one, I in them, and you in me, so that they may be completely one and that the world may see that you have sent me and love them as you love me. Father, I want those, whom you have given me, to be with me wherever I am, that they may see my glory, which you have given me; for you loved me, before the world was formed. Righteous Father, the world does not know you; but I know you, and they have recognised that you have sent me. And I have made your name known to them and I shall proclaim it, so that the love, with which you love me, may be in them, and that I may be in them."

John 17, 22-26

Jesus' wish is a relationship with us.

The main work of mankind is to glorify God and to „relish" him forever.

This means:

A life lived for God glorifies Him. We strive towards God with all our being – heart, soul, mind, and strength. We rest in Christ and therefore act as he acts, in that we love others. Thereby we bring glory to his name and moreover enjoy the relationship, for which we were created initially.

Whoever wishes to live for God must now begin to search for the Holy Spirit. This means, not to turn towards mankind as we know it. A life for God means giving up oneself and to want the Will of God more than anything else. If we come closer to him and become better acquainted with him, his wishes will quite naturally become our own. As we then mature, our wish to obey God's commandments will grow, because our love for him will grow as well.

As Jesus said:
„If you love me, you shall obey my commandments."

John 14, 15

Decision and the end of mankind's illusion

Everything begins with the clear knowledge, that mankind had been seduced and lives without a compass. If; because of this; we recognise what is missing, we must all accept the offer of Jesus Christ.

This world must be left behind; and with it also all deceitfulness and all catastrophes. Each one of us bears the responsibility for everything and therefore has the responsibility to say THANK YOU for a life with centuries full of possibilities. Without graciousness we would have been extinguished in the embers of confusion and deception.

Now mankind is locked up in a long corridor. On one end of the corridor stands the door of the past ... it is closed ... it will never again open. All of mankind is in this corridor. At its other end there are two doors: a very large portal and a very narrow, small door. Even a child must almost hunch down in order to pass through it. One must look especially closely in order to recognise that there are two doors. This is a spiritual place, which is rendered visible here by words.

The spiritual corridor has an important significance for this world. Up until now, the door to the past was always open. We had the power by means of free will to choose freely through which of the three doors we wanted to pass. The spiritual attitude during our lifetime and at its end was decisive in determining our choice. Until our present time, 99 percent of all people chose the door to the past. They always went back, in order to come again for a better life. God gave them the choice before each reincarnation. However, he also gave them spiritual tools installed in the soul-body. The purpose of these was to insure that the godly spark in us would become the helmsman over our lives.

Every individual; every human-spirit being was shown a spiritual path. The Son of God, Jesus, the Christ, breathed his spirit (a spirit particle) into the soul-spirit of every human-spirit being.

„I am the way, the truth and the life.“

We all carry this knowledge within us; every one of us. However, due to the fact that earthly life is extremely susceptible to temptation, only a small number of us decided to follow Jesus Christ. The churches carry a great deal of responsibility for this, due to their adulterated teachings about God, so that most of us followed either our own judgement, or temptation. We are seeing the results of this NOW!

We are now locked into the condition which WE allowed, which we created and which persists in us. Our souls are prisoners of the world; they no longer have the sensitivity in God; the spiritual relationship to God is lifeless and uncertain. No foundation in the rock.

The human spirit wanders around and has a confused undergrowth of thoughts within it, as well as an impoverished spiritual attitude. However, people the world over have begun slowly to unravel certain confusions. In centuries of lifetimes, this has happened now.

The safe harbour

God is the helmsman of all creation; he gave us the rudder. Jesus Christ is the sea upon which we sail. Mankind is the ship. All of us are invited by God to come into the safe harbour - and this is now being achieved.

There is no turning back, the ship can only progress in one direction; it must pass through the proper door. The sea is more turbulent than it has ever been. Everyone is longing for peace and quiet.

The spiritual condition, in which mankind finds itself, seeks liberation, conversion and awareness; which leads to the final commitment to the helmsman. If one speaks of illusion, it is here: Jesus Christ is the sea ... Thus he is the way, the truth and the life. We are the ship. Therefore we are sailing in Jesus Christ all the time. Nonetheless - because we are unaware of that fact and concentrate our spirits on the horizon instead of on our spiritual water - we live in the illusion that the sea is turbulent and full of danger.

God urges us to observe closely. Human, recognise:

When we do this, we turn our gaze introspectively and become aware of the illusion. Then we will immediately give our ship over to the sea; for Jesus Christ is the tranquil and safe water of our lives. He will bring us to the harbour of the eternal home.

Thus, everyone will reach these two doors; the large portal and the small, narrow door. If we choose Jesus in these distressing times in which we live, we will see that the small door leads us to spiritual peace.

If, however, we stay in the spirit of confusion and without Jesus in our spirits, we will once again be led into illusion; and that will cause us to choose the large portal. When this doorway opens, we will either enter into darkness for eternity, or – if we were to enter as doubters – we would have the forgiving chance to choose Jesus instantly.

That is everything in a nutshell. No further explanation is necessary.

The spiritual condition of the world is FAR FROM GOD. Now this condition is coming to an end, because the world is coming to an end. The house of the father in heaven is opened. Jesus is taking us home. Let us go with him.

Thanks be to HIM. So be it.

The New Jerusalem

"Then I saw a new heaven and a new earth; for the first heaven and the first earth had passed away, and there was no longer any sea.

And I saw the Holy City, the New Jerusalem, coming down out of heaven from God, prepared as a bride beautifully dressed for her husband.

And I heard a loud voice from the throne saying, Look! God's dwelling place is now among the people and he will dwell with them. They will be his people, and God himself will be with them and be their God. He will wipe every tear from their eyes.

There will be no more death or mourning or crying or pain, for the old order of things has passed away. And he who was seated on the throne said, "I am making everything new!"

Revelation 21, 1-5

The prayer of spiritual commitment to Jesus Christ

„Dear Lord Jesus,
I believe that You are the Son of God, died for our sins on the cross, and rose again on the third day.

I now come to You.

I wish to be the servant of sin no longer and distance myself from all works of darkness. I now rebuke Satan and all his offers in this world.

I distance myself from the empty, spirit- and fruitless gifts of the enemy of my soul.

Therefore, in belief in Your victory over the devil, death and sin, I lay down my „former person" at the foot of the cross.

Please forgive me my trespasses and help me to forgive those who have hurt me.
I, too, wish to forgive those who have sinned against me and will not impute them for their trespasses; because You have forgiven me.

Lord, please help me to forgive all those who have inflicted great physical or emotional pain upon me.

I give myself into Your hands; for I know that You are the only, true and living God. You are the only God, who is capable of healing my soul from all these misdeeds. I now lay down my former, sinful life.

Lord, Jesus Christ, please make me into a new creation.

Strengthen my faith; give me a new spirit and a new heart.

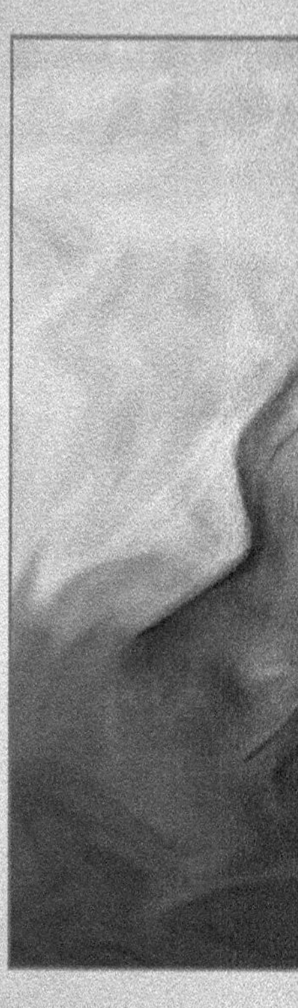

Give me eternal life and lead me through Your Holy Spirit into all truth.

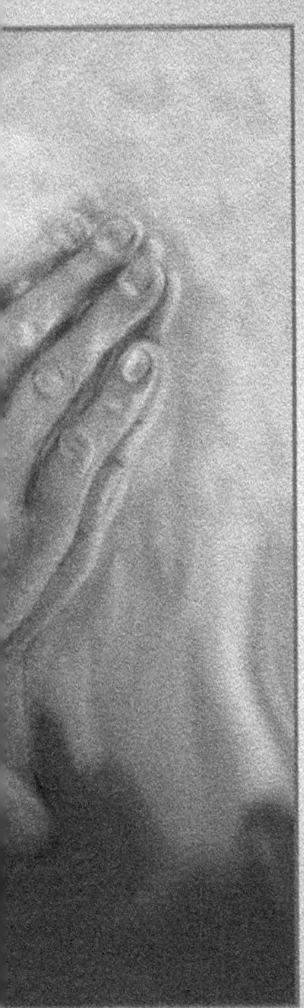

I will trust You from now on and I will live according to Your word.

Jesus Christ, please create a new heart within me and give me a new spirit and be the Lord of my life.

Lead me by means of Your spirit into all of truth and write my name in the book of life.

Thank You for washing me clean from all sin with your blood.

Jesus Christ, please glorify yourself in my life, which now belongs to You.

In the name of Jesus - Amen."

Your home

God is everything.

Whoever has bathed in his presence once, is lost forever to this world. A heavenly state will fill the spirit and soul. In this condition, one can even descend into so-called hell. If we find our selves in our self-created misery with God, we will be able to heal our suffering. To be healed in God is an eternal condition. If we apply other sources of alleviation, the relief will not last; for the eternal goblet alone holds eternal healing.

The spirit and soul of man must sense God together; for only then will all positive spiritual strengths be unfettered and the way home can begin, leading to freedom in this exhausting and wayward world. If you have been embraced and caressed by your dearest person, then you know the pleasurable feeling of being accepted and secure.

No number of this world suffices, if we would wish to multiply what sensation is called up by the touch of God. This world cannot express our Father in words. The translation of God is „the incomprehensible“. Since mankind always seeks the proof of things, the loss of not being able to experience God is an enormous wound.

Opening ourselves to the incomprehensible ... going with Jesus. He was tangible and real. His legacy exists in this world. His body left traces through his spilled blood. If we wish to go to God, we must first meet his son, trust him, entrust ourselves to him. Then we can embark on a safe path.

Approaching the end of this book let it be said: if you ever encounter a person who says that you can heal all misery within you by yourself; and that you need neither Jesus nor God, because you yourself are godly; know this:

You will then remain imprisoned in this world. The exit from all suffering is the small, narrow door. Open it and enter the spirit in Jesus.

Peace is.

How can one lone person help?

Most of us do not know what we can do for this world. We search desperately for our abilities to make ourselves useful.

The helplessness in us can give way to power. This force, however, should carry justice; and the deeds and words it employs should reflect this fairness. The Good News (the Bible) contains many righteous words which show us that when we enter into a relationship with God, we can become righteous even after having been unjust ourselves.

When we pray, we turn to God. We ask for something and God should fulfil our requests.

However, if we ourselves act out of our own godly strength, then we can put an end to the falseness and injustice, and instil repentance, through the power of proclamation.

What is a proclamation and how do we employ it?

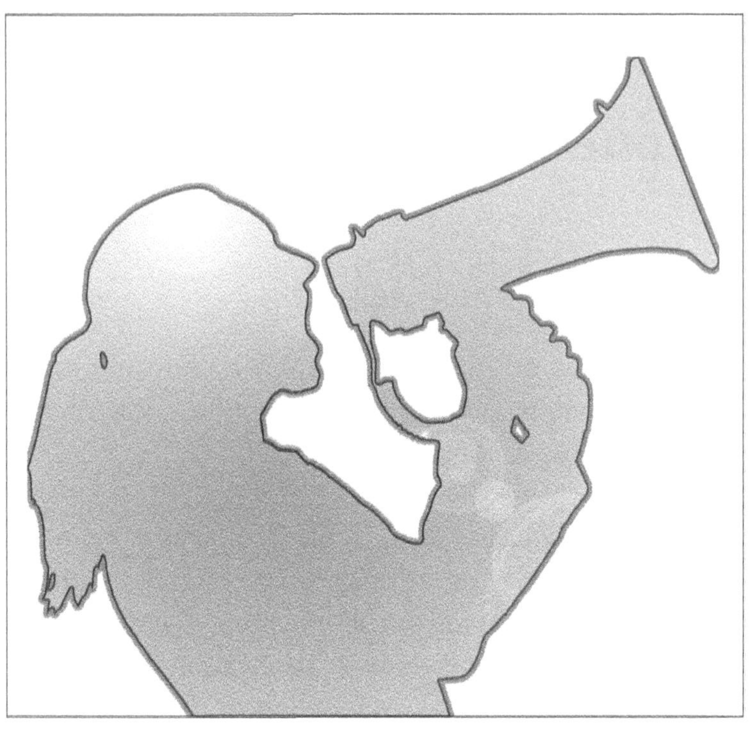

A proclamation is a courageous, public declaration or statement, spoken aloud, out of the truth and righteousness of God. It is the strongest possibility of releasing the Spirit of God.

Jesus said: „I am the way, the truth and the life."

If you wish to reach your neighbours with a reminder that they should follow Jesus; that he is the salvation of this world, you can call out: *„Jesus is our way, the truth and the life."*

„I have written you, because you are strong and the WORD OF GOD remains in you, and you have overcome evil."

1 John 2, 14

With a proclamation we release the good. We call it out, as did in times past the herald, the town crier.

You must put in the effort to search the Bible for suitable passages which should be used as your proclamation.

I give you here a strong declaration against everything evil, against plagues, pandemics and illnesses:

„Therefore put on the full armour of GOD ... Stand firm then, with the belt of truth buckled around your waist, with the breastplate of righteousness in place, and with your feet fitted with the readiness that comes from the gospel of peace ... the shield of faith, with which you can extinguish all the flaming arrows of the evil one ... the helmet of salvation and the sword of the Spirit, which is the WORD OF GOD."

Ephesians 6, 13-17

Further Proclamations:

In the power of having donned God's armour, by the efficacy of might; by the strength of God through Jesus Christ; I now proclaim freedom for humanity. The evil of this world is repealed.

In the name of Christ I bind all dark and unjust forces and call them back in the name of Jesus Christ.

In the name of Jesus Christ I bind the spirit of lies and deceit.

In the name of Jesus Christ I activate all heavenly messengers and helpers of God, my Father, so that they may deprive all evil forces of power and push them back to where Jesus commands them.

I activate the spirit of the truth of God, so that it may inundate all creatures in and on the Earth; and that truth shall be the only ruling power.

„We are of God, and whoever knows God, listens to us; whoever is not of God, does not listen to us. This is how we recognise the Spirit of Truth and the Spirit of Error.“

1 John 4, 6

All problems and all situations of mankind can be transformed in this manner. Go and grasp this great possibility to become finally a co-creator through the word of God, through Jesus Christ, through righteousness and truth.

May you all be blessed in Jesus Christ.

Afterword

If you wish to experience this book consciously and regard your own life - as well as the state of the world - you will recognise quickly, that mankind needs the connection to God and Jesus Christ, in order to experience the spiritual justice which leads to long-awaited peace. This is certain!

„We know that a person is not justified by the works of the law, but by faith in Jesus Christ. So we, too, have put our faith in Christ Jesus that we may be justified by faith in Christ and not by the works of the law, because by the works of the law no one will be justified."

Galatians 2, 16

About the Author

Andrea Regina Katharina InEssenz is an original Christian mystic of contemporary times. She lives a mystical life and helps people to find access to God once again. This occurs by means of the spiritual fire of love, which operates through Andrea as a beneficial power for mankind. Andrea's healing is - through her deep connection to Jesus Christ - primarily Christian and essential.

A good, true sage will show you time and time again where you are still unaware.

A true leader is concerned with your shadows; for they are the causes of your suffering. They have fallen away from love and grope around in darkness.

The sage illuminates what is essential for them. Consequently, the journey home begins for the soul. Light of Light ... So be it!

Encounters with Andrea

The great love of God flows through Andrea's body into the outside world and thereby helps all beings; human and animal alike; to attain personal transformation. The proximity of God is the point act of delivery, and is bestowed through the presence – the pure being – of Andrea.

The path to annexation into human nature placed a veil over free, spiritual strength and caused forgetfulness of that which is TRUE. Thereby a new spiritual world arose – the visible world, which every individual perceives and helps to shape. This is, however, merely a copy of an impermeable spirit and needs to be cleansed and clarified, and to return to the pure source. This is the longing of mankind.

Andrea's great mission is to let us experience our own light again. This happens through Christ and God Himself, both of whom manifest themselves through the mere presence of Andrea. Her existence here on Earth is an act of grace and a gift to all humanity.

The only wish Andrea Regina Katharina InEssenz has is:

„May a healthy spiritual attitude and intense love of God be given to all people. It is quite easy to love God, as he demands nothing ... he only wishes to be loved."

You can find contact, videos and the possibility of an encounter

with Andrea Regina Katharina InEssenz

on her website:

www.andrea-inessenz.de

Also available in English:

Many people search for the Royal Road in their lives. Numerous spiritual propositions - especially those of esoteric or shamanistic nature - claim to be able to offer the seeker a way of experiencing redemption or liberation. Is that the true Royal Road? How does one find it? In recent times the search for redemption has reached the collective human consciousness. Countless people are already underway to discover it. They have created many rituals, relics and writings in order to glimpse a spark of truth and light.

When all veils fall, faith can be experienced and becomes the only certainty. Here rests quintessential liberation and peace. Thus a person will be redeemed. The only true Royal Road is the path to our Creator, to God. His son Jesus Christ walked this path, as did other individuals thereafter.

This work is for all people: the unbelievers, churchgoers, and all spiritual seekers and practitioners. These writings will perhaps awaken or provoke outrage. Only the person who has opened a spark of truth within him-/herself, will - as though intoxicated - grasp the messages and use them for the good. For them these writings will be a shining light. Receiving the Father of all Creation into oneself and letting His presence mature into the truth is significantly more important than exalted feelings or the knowledge, which humanity so highly values.

Royal Road - Where are you? (Paperback)
ISBN 978-3949324-01-7 (February 2021 / 108 pages)

This book is meant to enhance cognisance.

There is but one truth to be recognised:
We are children of God and carry within us the power - which was given us by Him - to reveal the errors of this world and to overcome them.

There is only one path to this end:
„I am the way, the truth and the life."

Jesus, the Saviour the Christ

This world has been seduced by dark forces. What these are, you will find in the contents of this book

Whoever can allow themselves to absorb the message, will awaken from a long sleep. The spirit needs living nourishment! The time for it is NOW.

This book can be the key you have always sought.
Dare to find it and then use it, so that you can overcome this world and its suffering, and enter into the peace of God.

That is the purpose of your life - that is why you are a human being!
May peace be with you.

The Seven World-Demons and Salvation through Jesus, the CHRIST (Paperback)
ISBN 978-3949324-07-9 (October 2021 / 124 pages)

The Child-Father relationship to God is a natural state inherent in the spirit and soul of every human being.

Through the mystical path of the authoress - which was so deeply moved by God's spiritual fire, that all separation between her and God was removed - she explains in wisdom the true path of every soul. Her method of expression shows that she is one with God and bears no dogmas.

This book contains the truth about human development and frees the reader from errors and erroneous conditioning. By means of the mystic's perception as elucidated in this book, the reader can enter the level of true existence: the soul, which carries eternal life. Profound insights and veracity are the gifts of this work, which was written in the name of God.

Thus the reader can build a new relationship with him-/herself, with his or her soul and with God - as well as recognising that Christ is the way to peace.

The True Life of the Soul (Paperback)
ISBN 978-3949324-06-2 (May 2021 / 192 pages)

These books by the author are available
in bookstores, by amazon.com or amazon.co.uk or at edition inessenz: **www.andrea-inessenz.de**

Walk with Jesus - Mankind returns to God

1st edition 2021

(Original Title: Geh mit Jesus - Der Mensch kehrt um zu Gott)
Translated from German by Vincenzo Benestante

Editor / Author:	Andrea InEssenz
Cover design, typesetting & layout:	Roland H-P Lutz
ISBN 978-3-949324-10-9 (Paperback)	
Credit:	
page 38 & inside back cover	Roland H-P Lutz
page 28 Fabijenna Wagner / page 30 Marion Ohmer Title page 3 & 20 Karin Henseler / page 4 Stefan Keller / page 10 Comfreak / page 12 & 24 Gerd Altmann / page 15 Pete Linforth / page 16 Mystic Art Design / page 34 Mohamed Hassan	all Pixabay

On the author's website you will find more current, especially mystical texts. Visit for this:

www.andrea-inessenz.de or follow her on:
facebook: / Andreainessenz ¶ twitter: / Andreainessenz
vimeo: / andreainessenz ¶ youtube: // Andrea InEssenz

www.ingramcontent.com/pod-product-compliance
Ingram Content Group UK Ltd.
Pitfield, Milton Keynes, MK11 3LW, UK
UKHW021643190726
13853UKWH00001B/27